RAF FIGHTERS 1918-1937 a pictorial survey

RAF FIGHTERS

1918 ~ 1937

G. R. DUVAL AFM

D. BRADFORD BARTON LIMITED

Frontispiece: The Bristol Bulldog was the most widely used R.A.F. fighter type of the inter-war period, serving from 1929 to 1937 in ten Squadrons. The Bulldog also served with the R.A.A.F. and the Air Forces of Sweden, Estonia, Latvia, Denmark and Finland. The re-built example shown here over Farnborough featured in many air displays, but was eventually wrecked in a crash at the 1963 Farnborough Air Show.

 © copyright D. Bradford Barton Ltd 1975   *ISBN 0 85153 208 X*

printed in Great Britain by H. E. Warne Ltd, London and St. Austell

for the publishers

D. BRADFORD BARTON LTD · **Trethellan House** · **Truro** · **Cornwall** · **England**

foreword

It may be said with truth that this book depicts the "Golden Age" of the biplane in Royal Air Force Fighter Squadron service, and as such provides an interesting comparison to the recently published volume on American fighters of the same period. In the present supersonic age, this type of aircraft is all but extinct, and the modern fighter is becoming more and more of a piloted missile, severely functional and with little character, but in those far-off inter-war years the reverse was the case, and those times and machines hold great interest for the enthusiast and a strong nostalgia for ex-servicemen with long memories. Each machine was an individual, with its own idiosyncrasies, carefully rigged to pilot's requirements and maintained in a state of immaculate cleanliness and high polish. While this might be considered excessive, it should be remembered that the pride and efficiency, together with the spirit and rivalry of those days, was instrumental in the victory of 1940.

My publisher and I would like to take this opportunity to record our thanks to the Ministry of Defence, the Bristol and Hawker Siddeley Companies, and Mr Bruce Robertson, for their assistance in the preparation of this book.

Watton
Norfolk

G. R. DUVAL

A Gloster Grebe of No. 25 Squadron. This type replaced the wartime Sopwith Snipes.

The Armstrong Whitworth Siskin III entered service in 1924, and the second production aircraft is seen here. Despite its somewhat ungainly appearance, the Siskin was a highly manoeuvrable aircraft, and a regular performer at the popular Hendon Air Displays in the hands of No. 41 Squadron pilots from Northolt.

introduction

On April 1st, 1918, the Royal Air Force officially came into being as an amalgamation of the Royal Flying Corps and the Royal Naval Air Service. Oddly enough, the German Air Force was a prime mover in this formation, as their daylight raids on London of June and July 1917 had caused such a public outcry that General Smuts was appointed to produce recommendations from a searching examination of Britain's Air Defence organisation, the subsequent report advocating unification of the R.F.C. and R.N.A.S. and the expansion of the Air Board into a full Air Ministry as a Department of State. These recommendations received Royal Assent at the end of November 1917, and a very worthy choice was made by appointing Major-General Sir Hugh Trenchard, *K.C.B., D.S.O.,* as the first Chief of the Air Staff.

At the time of its formation, the R.A.F. was the most powerful air force in the world, with the main bulk of its fighter strength comprising Sopwith Camels, Bristol Fighters, and S.E.5As. In the last great battles of World War I, these were joined by a small number of newer types, such as the Sopwith Snipe and Dolphin which, had the war continued, would have largely replaced the older aircraft. As the last months of 1918 passed, the attrition of the German Air Force and land forces gained momentum as massive formations of British and Allied fighters maintained air superiority patrols over the Western Front, also attacking German airfields in strength. In overseas theatres, too, the action was fierce, for September 1918 saw the virtual destruction of the Turkish Seventh Army in Palestine by R.A.F. fighters and bombers.

With the Armistice of November 1918, and massive demobilisation, the ascendancy of the R.A.F. was halted in dramatic fashion, and indeed, its whole future lay in the balance. On the one hand, the Army and the Navy put forward a case for the return of the Air Force to their respective controls, and on the other, some political circles argued on the "war to end all wars" platform, for total abandonment of air power. Throughout all this, Trenchard fought hard for retention of the R.A.F. as a separate force, and in the end, succeeded.

With the political and inter-Service battles over and won, a much reduced R.A.F. settled down to get used to its new uniforms and ranks, while post-war economies decreed the continued use of wartime aircraft, the Sopwith Snipe and the Bristol Fighter being selected as the standard fighters. There might have been just one new aircraft type for the fighter Squadrons in the Nieuport Nighthawk, but for the failure of the much heralded A.B.C. Dragonfly radial engine, which had been selected for standard use and ordered in quantity. As it was, the Snipe continued in use with fighter Squadrons until as late as 1926, and the Bristol Fighter was finally retired in 1932.

By March, 1920, the number of R.A.F. Squadrons had risen from the all-time low of twelve in 1919 to an encouraging twenty-five, of which a good proportion were fighters. Also in 1920, the R.A.F. played its part in putting down the activities of the "Mad Mullah" in Somaliland, the first Hendon Air Display was staged before 60,000 spectators, and last but not least, the R.A.F. College at Cranwell opened. All of this was good publicity for the Service, and more was to follow in 1922 when the military control for Iraq was placed entirely in the hands of the R.A.F., the first of several such commands.

In 1923 it was becoming apparent that the Snipe could not go on for ever, and with a few more funds available, the Air Ministry placed orders for a moderate number of replacement fighter aircraft. There were two types, the Armstrong Whitworth Siskin and the Gloster Grebe, both powered by the Armstrong Siddeley Jaguar engine, and these machines were to set the fashion of radial-engined R.A.F. biplane fighters which lasted until the late 1930s. Apart from the

lift to morale occasioned by the arrival of these new aircraft at their designated units in 1924, the Siskin and Grebe were the first machines to bear the colourful Squadron markings which became a feature of all Fighter Squadrons from then on. It is true that during World War I, unit markings had been applied, but these had been of a very restricted nature and anything of a flamboyant nature severely frowned upon. Now, the use of coloured Squadron identification was officially authorised, and with it, as had doubtless been foreseen, came a resurgence of friendly but intense inter-Squadron rivalry in every field from flying efficiency to sporting activity. At this time, the use of the first oxygen and radio-telephone systems began to increase, together with experiments in heated flying clothing, and at long last the wearing of parachutes became mandatory. With this latter innovation, the fighter pilots could now safely fly their machines to the limit, which they did with zest, and so began the aerobatic and formation displays that thrill spectators to the present day. An early example of what was to come occurred at the 1925 Hendon Display, when the Grebes of No. 25 Squadron performed formation aerobatics directed from the ground by radio-telephony Royal Command in the form of the voice of H.M. King George V.

1925 saw the arrival of the Hawker Woodcock to replace the ageing Snipes of No. 3 and 17 Squadrons, and this was the first single-seat fighter to be produced by this famous Company. It was also the first post-war R.A.F. fighter to be officially designated as a night-fighter, for which duty it was admirably suited. No. 3 Squadron lost no time in demonstrating their prowess, giving a display of night flying at the 1926 Birmingham Torchlight Tattoo with their aircraft in formation fitted with batteries of under-wing electric lamps. The Woodcock also introduced the efficient Bristol Jupiter engine for the first time in a British fighter aircraft. Another newcomer was shown for the first time in the New Types Park at the 1925 Hendon Display, also powered by a Jupiter engine. This was the superb little Gloster Gamecock, developed from the Grebe, which it was intended to replace, and notable as the last biplane fighter of wooden construction to serve with the R.A.F. The Gamecock equipped five Squadrons, which were developed to a high state of efficiency in the operational side of the home-based R.A.F., now re-organised as the Air Defences of Great Britain, embodying a Bombing Area, a Fighting Area, a Special Reserve, and the beginnings of the Auxiliary Air Force—the "Weekend Fliers". The first

Squadrons of this excellent and useful Force were formed in 1925 with light bombers, but later became fighter units. Under the new organisation, all fighter Squadrons were home-based; the last to serve operationally overseas on a permanent basis was No. 1, with Snipes, and they returned to Britain in 1927 to re-equip with Siskins.

In 1927, No. 41 and No. 1 Squadrons were the first of an eventual total of ten units to be equipped with the Siskin IIIA which, despite the similarity of Mark number, was a very different aircraft from the 1924 model, being faster and much cleaner aerodynamically and, powered with a supercharged Jaguar engine, had a Service ceiling of 27,000 feet. For high-altitude flight, the pilot was provided with oxygen from a liquid-oxygen tank, although in practice flights over 16,000 feet were the exception rather than the rule. A superb aerobatic aircraft, the Siskin IIIA featured at every Hendon Air Display from 1927 to 1931, and was a milestone in development as the first R.A.F. fighter of all-metal construction.

Up to this time, the various types of fighter aircraft in service with the R.A.F. had not shown any significant increase in performance over the Snipe of World War I, and what increase there had been was in most part due to the development of higher-powered engines. In the Annual Air Exercises, the current fighter types found little difficulty in intercepting slow and cumbersome bombers such as the Vickers Virginia and the Fairey Fawn. However, in 1926, just one light bomber Squadron, No. 12, was equipped with the Fairey Fox, powered by the Curtiss D-12 in-line engine, and these aircraft evaded all the fighter defences in exercises for the simple reason that their performance equalled that of the Siskin and exceeded that of the Gamecock. This fact impelled the fighter designers to greater effort, and a number of prototypes were put forward to meet an Air Ministry Specification for a Gamecock/Siskin replacement. The type chosen was the Bristol Bulldog, which, ordered in quantity, was to equip ten Squadrons from 1929 to 1936, comprising at the height of its service some seventy per cent of United Kingdom air defences in the fighter sector. Altogether, three hundred and two Bulldogs were supplied to the R.A.F., plus fifty-eight dual control trainers, all powered by an improved Mark of Bristol Jupiter engine. The Bulldog had a maximum speed of 174 m.p.h., which was considered adequate to deal with light bombers such as the Fox and other light bombers extant in the world's Air Forces. For all this, in 1930, the superbly-adaptable Hawker Hart light bomber appeared, with a maximum speed of 184 m.p.h. It was all too obvious that light bomber development was outstripping that of the fighter, and if it was happening in Britain it could well happen elsewhere. The Air Ministry were in a quandary, for considerable finance had been allocated to quantity production of the Bulldog, selected as the R.A.F. standard fighter. However, a Specification had been issued for an aircraft to fill a new role, that of interceptor fighter, and two machines had been put forward; the Fairey Firefly and the Hawker Hornet, both representing a radical change in design study influenced by the Fox and the Hart in that both had in-line engines of low frontal area. In the event, the Hornet was chosen as the R.A.F. standard interceptor fighter and re-named Fury; the current financial situation dictating equipment of three Squadrons only, to act as the air defence spearhead.

A beautiful aircraft, and by far the most elegant of all biplane fighters to serve with the R.A.F., the Fury I received so much publicity, both in the aviation press and by superb performances at the Hendon and other air displays, that the impression was given of almost total R.A.F. fighter equipment with the type, which was certainly not so, and only one hundred and seventeen were ever built of this Mark. It is true that the Fury II, a more powerful version with the Kestrel VI engine, appeared in 1936 to equip the original Squadrons plus two more, but again, only ninety-eight were built, and their performance, good though it was, fell below that of their immediate successor, the Gloster Gauntlet.

The adaptability of the Hawker Hart light bomber has already been mentioned, and in 1931 it was decided to introduce a two-seat fighter variant for the R.A.F., thus providing a successor to the famous Bristol Fighter in the last years of its long service. The Hart Fighter, re-named Demon in 1932, was eventually to equip a total of eleven Squadrons, of which five were Auxiliary Air Force. For its time, the Demon had a useful performance, with a maximum speed of 182 m.p.h., and in 1935 two Squadrons, together with one Squadron of Bulldogs, became the first R.A.F. fighters despatched for possible active service overseas since the 1920s, when they went to the Middle East during the Abyssinian crisis. From October 1936, the Demon was fitted with a Frazer-Nash hydraulic gunner's turret, partly for protection of the gunner by armour-plate but mainly because operation of a free gun in an open cockpit was becoming extremely difficult as speeds increased.

By 1936, with the rising strength of the German Luftwaffe and the belligerence of Japan in the Far East, the adequacy of the current expansion plans for the R.A.F. was in question, and in February of that year the target was raised to a total of 1,736 first-line aircraft of all types by March 1939. As far as fighters were concerned, the prototypes of the new monoplanes, the Spitfire and Hurricane, had already flown, but the setting up of quantity production would take time. The urgency for re-equipment of the R.A.F.'s new Fighter Command, set up on 14th July 1936, was heavily underlined by the events of the Spanish Civil War, when Germany and Italy, and Russia, demonstrated their latest combat aircraft in support of their separate ideals. It was now apparent that the era of biplane fighters in the R.A.F. was fast drawing to a close, and that any new types of this configuration would have to be of high performance as a stop-gap until arrival of the Hurricane and Spitfire in the fighter Squadrons.

The current fighter type in 1936 was the Gloster Gauntlet, introduced in the previous year to succeed the Bulldog, a number of which were still in service. The Gauntlet, with a Bristol Mercury engine, was the last open-cockpit R.A.F. fighter and the fastest yet produced, with its maximum speed of 230 m.p.h. It was considered by pilots to be the best of all biplane fighters in all-round capability, which included a take-off distance of 100 yards, with just 50 yards more required for landing, and a climb to 20,000 feet in 9 minutes. Twenty Squadrons were equipped with the Gauntlet, and, with others, experienced the upheaval of the 'Munich Crisis of 1938 which, however intentioned, gave the R.A.F. one more precious year to prepare for what was certainly to come. On September 3rd 1939, one Squadron, No. 616 (South Yorkshire) still had Gauntlets, retaining them until Spitfires arrived in October. However, the Gauntlet, before its passing, helped to forge one link in the chain of defeat for the Luftwaffe during the Battle of Britain, for under conditions of utmost secrecy, a Section of No. 32 Squadron's aircraft were directed to make the first airborne interception by radar in November 1936, directed from Bawdsey Manor.

The last R.A.F. biplane fighter was the Mercury-powered Gladiator, and it is perhaps fitting that this aircraft achieved fame in the early days of a war belonging to high-performance monoplanes. With an enclosed cabin, four-gun armament, and the refinement of flaps, the Gladiator had a maximum speed of 253 m.p.h. and a high degree of manoeuvrability. The first Gladiators were issued to No. 3 Squadron in March 1937, eventually forming the equipment of twenty-three more Squadrons; although largely replaced in Fighter Command by the outbreak of war, they served with distinction in France, equipped one Squadron (No. 247) during the Battle of Britain, scored some of the war's earliest victories in defence of the Shetlands, and fought actions in Greece and the Western Desert. Probably the most famous Gladiator exploits were the operations against the Luftwaffe by No. 263 Squadron from a frozen Norwegian lake, and the defence of Malta in the early days by three ex-Sea Gladiators.

9

Personnel and S.E.5 aircraft of No. 1 Squadron at Clarmarais, on the Western Front, in July 1918. This appears to be one of the few photographs on which the aircraft serial numbers were not obliterated by the censor. Close study reveals a variety of uniforms, including those of the new R.A.F. and the original R.F.C. plus some mixtures!

A post-war S.E.5A, photographed on 21 November 1919. Together with the Sopwith Camel, this aircraft was a leading type in fighter service during World War I, and was flown by many well-known fighter pilots with considerable success. A number of S.E.5As remained in use for a short period after the Armistice, and were then scrapped.

The famous Sopwith Camel formed the equipment of no less than thirty-two R.A.F. Squadrons in October 1918, and was responsible for the destruction of many enemy aircraft. The 73 Squadron aircraft shown here survived a mid-air collision, possibly due to the horse-shoe motif. Few Camels survived the post-war R.A.F. reorganisation.

The Sopwith Pup was one of the most popular British fighter aircraft of World War I, and after its introduction in 1916 was built in large numbers. Replaced by the Camel, the Pup finished its war service as a trainer.

A Sopwith Camel of No. 208 Squadron, R.A.F. after a forced landing near Cherisy, on the Western Front. With the formation of the Royal Air Force on 1 April 1918, all the incorporated R.N.A.S. Squadrons had 200 added to their numbers; thus this aircraft originally belonged to No. 8 Naval Squadron.

An immaculate Wolseley-built S.E.5A in factory-fresh condition. The engine was a 200 h.p. Wolseley W.4A Viper, which was installed as a result of problems with the earlier Hispano-Suiza unit. Later S.E.5As were fitted with strengthened front undercarriage struts.

An unarmed Sopwith Camel fitted with additional mid-bay rigging wires. This aircraft was the first British fighter to carry twin machine guns, and its name was derived from the "hump" fairing over these guns. The Camel was not an easy machine to fly, due to the gyroscopic effect of its rotary engine and a short fuselage.

When the Bristol Fighter was introduced in the spring of 1917, several casualties were suffered due to its use in tight formations, but as soon as pilots realised that it could, and should, be flown aggressively, it proved to be a very successful aircraft in action, serving with the R.A.F. until 1932.

Sopwith Snipe F2485 flying over Constantinople in 1922 from the 25 Squadron base at San Stefano. This was during the Turko-Greek conflict known as the Chanak crisis, when several R.A.F. units were sent to reinforce the British garrison in Constantinople. Two years earlier, the Snipes of No. 25 formed the only operational fighter Squadron in the U.K.

A line-up of Sopwith Snipes in post-war silver finish. Powered by the 230 h.p. Bentley B.R.2 engine, the Snipe was designed in 1917 as a Camel replacement, Squadron deliveries being made in the late summer of 1918. The Snipe remained in R.A.F. service as a fighter and fighter-trainer until withdrawn in 1927.

The fourth and final Sopwith Dolphin prototype, flown to France in October 1917. The Dolphin saw limited service on the Western Front, and had a good high-altitude performance coupled with excellent manoeuvrability, but suffered from engine problems and pilots' doubts regarding crash survival in a nose-over situation.

17

Early 1920s airfield scene as Snipes are prepared for the day's flying programme. The machine in the foreground is contract-built by the Nieuport & General Aircraft Company, who delivered 100 Snipes in the postwar period, while the aircraft on the end of the line is one of the 40-odd two-seater trainer variants.

Immediately after the war, Hugh Trenchard (later Viscount, Marshal of the Royal Air Force) set up the School of Technical Training for Apprentices at Halton. A group of the young "Trenchard's Brats" are seen here on 2 January 1921 with a Snipe aircraft.

Snipe E6837 of No. 5 Flying Training School, photographed in 1927. Pupil pilots completed their initial training on the Avro 504K before passing to the Snipe Flights, and once they had got used to the gyroscopic effect of a large rotary engine, and the mixture handling, found it a very pleasant aircraft to fly.

n excellent view of a Snipe amed "Bonzo") being run-up a Flying School. The two rmen are waiting to pull away the ocks, while a third holds down e tail in a slipstream-blast avily laced with castor oil mes. The wooden wheel-chock s in use for over fifty years!

No. 1 Squadron Snipes in formation over Iraq. The unit was based at Hinaidi from 1921 to 1926 for policing work generally connected with tribal wars and rebellions, the R.A.F. having assumed responsibility for the security of the country in 1922.

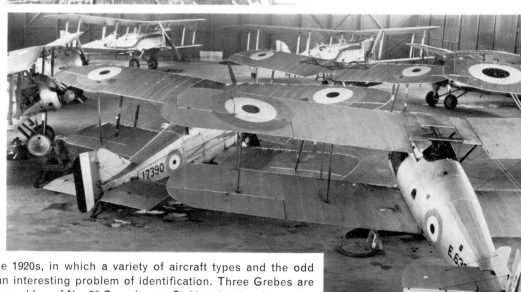

A typical hangar scene of the 1920s, in which a variety of aircraft types and the odd Squadron marking presents an interesting problem of identification. Three Grebes are present, one with the red cross and bar of No. 29 Squadron, a Siskin wingtip shows the red bar of No. 41 Squadron, and the Snipes may have belonged to either unit. D.H.9As are in the background.

A Jaguar-engined Nieuport Nighthawk flying over Hinaidi, in Iraq, during operational trials with No. 1 Squadron in 1923. Construction and development of a small batch of Nighthawks were taken over by the Gloucestershire (later Gloster) company, and the type has significance as the first post-war R.A.F. fighter to employ a radial engine, and the first of a long line of Service biplane fighters.

No. 1 Squadron received four Nighthawk aircraft in all, and was the only unit to operate the type. Nighthawk H8544 is seen here in flight, powered by a Jaguar engine. These aircraft were scheduled for quantity production, which was halted by the failure of the A.B.C. Dragonfly radial engine, their original power unit.

An excellent view of a Jaguar-engined Nighthawk with its ground crew, photographed at either Bangalore in India or Hinaidi, for these aircraft were with No. 1 Squadron at both bases. Below: a Nighthawk in the U.K., fitted with a Jupiter engine. This may well be J2405, which was fitted with a Bristol Jupiter II in 1922. Two Jupiter-powered aircraft went out to Hinaidi in 1923.

The Nieuport Nightjar was a Nighthawk variant for deck-landing duties, with a Bentley B.R.2 rotary engine. Twenty-two were built for the R.A.F. and served as land fighters with No. 203 Squadron during the Chanak crisis. The prototype is shown here, serialled H8535.

A Grebe in flight. This small fighter was immensely popular in the R.A.F., and apart from normal use featured in much early Service experimental work. It was the first fighter to survive a terminal velocity dive (at 240 m.p.h.), and in 1926 two Grebes were successfully air-launched from the R.33 airship at 2,000 feet.

Together with the Armstrong Whitworth Siskin, the Gloster Grebe was selected to re-equip R.A.F. Squadrons after World War I, and entered service with No. 111 Squadron at Duxford in 1923, powered by Armstrong Siddeley Jaguar IV engines. Illustrated is a production Grebe II of No. 25 Squadron, fitted with auxiliary struts to cure wing flutter.

A Grebe pilot of
No. 25 Squadron
displays flying
clothing *circa* 1925.
Parachutes had just
been issued for the
first time (this one
appears to be an
American Irvin), a
liquid oxygen system
was in use, and radio-
telephony was in the
early stages of
development. This pilot
incongruously wears
ordinary service-
pattern shoes!

A line-up of No. 25 Squadron Grebes, bearing their distinctive Squadron marking of two parallel black bars. This photograph was taken during a visit to the Gloster works airfield at Brockworth, the unit being led by the C.O., Sqn. Ldr. A. H. Peck, *DSO MC,* having flown from their base at Hawkinge. No. 25 were equipped with Grebes from 1924 to 1929.

An immaculate Grebe on the tarmac. These, and subsequent aircraft of the inter-war period, were maintained in a pristine condition of high polish and colourful decor.

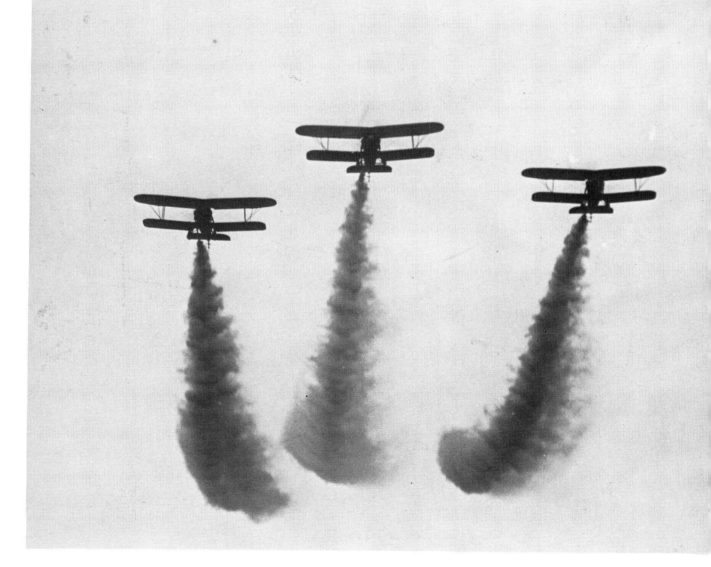

A Grebe, bearing the red and white checks of No. 56 Squadron, in an undignified pose after a landing mishap. This aircraft, J7535, was one of a batch of two-seaters built in 1925 for pilot conversion. Another two-seater, J7520, flew in the 1928 King's Cup Air Race with a broken flying-wire repaired by string!

◄

The Grebe was finally superseded by the Siskin in the summer of 1928, but a farewell performance was given at the 1931 Hendon Air Display by three machines from the Aeroplane and Armament Experimental Establishment at Martlesham Heath, using coloured smoke to enhance their aerobatics.

Another No. 17 Squadron Woodcock, J7971, with its black zig-zag Squadron marking. Replaced by Siskins and Gamecocks in 1928, the Woodcock had one more claim to fame, for a No. 17 Squadron machine was loaned to Col. Lindbergh for the flight back to Paris from London on 2 June 1927, soon after his transatlantic flight.

The Hawker Woodcock was one of the lesser known R.A.F. fighters of the inter-war years, but was significant as the first single-seater fighter from the Hawker Company, and the first R.A.F. machine specifically to be designated as a night fighter. A No. 17 machine, J7960, is shown here. The Woodcock also equipped No. 3 Squadron.

This head-on view of the Woodcock shows some of its night-flying equipment, including navigation and formation lights, under-wing flare brackets, and guns mounted on the fuselage sides to screen muzzle flash. The engine was a 420 h.p. Bristol Jupiter IV. The wide-track undercarriage made for stable take-offs and landings at night.

A Vic formation of No. 3 Squadron Woodcocks taking off at Upavon, the unit base for ten years, 1924-1934. The Squadron marking was a green band along the fuselage, and between the roundels on the top wing. Both No. 3 and No. 17 received Woodcocks in the late spring of 1925, and at once began intensive night-flying practice.

The Hawker Dancock was a modified version of the R.A.F. Woodcock for Danish Navy use, and three Hawker-built machines equipped 2 *Luftflotille* upon its formation at Ringsted in 1926. A further twelve Dancocks were built in Denmark under licence. The Dancock was fitted with a Jupiter IV engine, and racks for light bombs.

The last biplane fighter of wooden construction to serve with the R.A.F., the Gloster Gamecock was powered by a 425 h.p. Bristol Jupiter VI engine, and, like the earlier S.E.5 and Grebe, was designed by H. P. Folland. The first production Gamecocks were issued to No. 23 Squadron at Henlow in May 1926.

A Gamecock in flight, bearing the black and white check markings of No. 43 Squadron, known throughout the Service as the "Fighting Cocks" from their Squadron badge, designed to commemorate issue of this aircraft type. No. 43 received its Gamecocks in 1926 at Henlow, then moved to Tangmere, where it re-equipped with Siskins in 1928.

Five R.A.F. Squadrons, Nos. 3, 17, 23, 32 and 43, were equipped with the Gamecock, and in this view No. 2
is shown on parade on a rather wet day at Kenley in 1927. The Squadron markings of No. 23 were alternate
red and blue squares, and the unit operated Gamecocks from April 1926 until re-equipment with Bulldogs
in July 1931.

One of 43 Squadron's Gamecocks displays its upper wing marking. As popular with the pilots as the Grebe
had been before it, the Gamecock was a star performer at the Hendon Air Displays up to 1931, showing off
its superlative aerobatic capability. During test flights, the Gamecock achieved 275 m.p.h. in a dive, and
recovered from 22-turn spins.

On a somewhat better day, No. 23 Squadron poses for its photograph in an unusual but
not unique formation, with all fifteen Gamecocks on parade. Inter-Squadron rivalry and
competition were very strong in those days, pervading every aspect of Service life from
sport to gunnery scores, hence this type of photograph!

Ground view of a No. 43 Squadron Gamecock. It may be noted that the aircraft is fitted with navigation lights for night-flying, which by now had become a regular practice for single-seater Squadrons. The Gamecock was armed with two Vickers machine-guns, positioned in blast troughs, low on the fuselage sides.

A No. 43 Squadron Gamecock at Tangmere, with its ground crew. Unlike some fighters the Gamecock was relatively easy to service, for a good deal of thought had been given to accessibility at the design stage, and detachable panels were positioned in all the right places. The fuel tanks were situated in the upper wing.

A late-production Gamecock of unknown unit. Eighty-two Gamecocks were built for the R.A.F., and a number were also built for the Finnish Air Force, who frequently operated them on skis in winter.

The Gloster G.19 Guan was an experimental high-altitude fighter, developed from the Gamecock and fitted with a supercharged Napier Lion VI engine driving an adjustable-pitch propeller. The exhaust-driven supercharger was mounted above the propeller shaft, an arrangement also employed in American experiments.

The Hawker Hornbill of 1926 was an unsuccessful competitor for adoption as a Service fighter type, but is interesting as the first post-war design to mount an in-line engine, the Rolls-Royce Condor. Much of the design work had been done by Sidney Camm, later responsible for the Fury and Hurricane fighters.

The Vickers 161, built to A.M. Specification F29/27 and powered by a Bristol Jupiter engine, was one of many experimental types tested at Martlesham Heath for possible Service use. Of most unusual layout, the Vickers 161 was armed with a Coventry Ordnance Works 37 mm. quick-firing gun. This machine was not adopted.

The Hawker Hawfinch of 1927 was built to A.M. Specification F.20/27, as were prototypes from other companies, among which was the Bristol Bulldog. The Hawfinch was powered by a 530 h.p. Bristol Jupiter VIIF engine, and was designed by W. G. Carter. The Bulldog was awarded a production contract, and the Hawfinch served Hawkers as an experimental aircraft until 1929.

Following the amalgamation in 1921 of Siddeley Deasey Motors and Armstrong Whitworth, the original Siddeley Siskin fighter of 1920 was progressively developed from the Mk. II through to Mk. V, all of which were civilian-registered and fitted with the Armstrong Siddeley Jaguar engine. An Air Ministry contract was placed for the Siskin Mk. III, this aircraft entering R.A.F. service in 1924. The second production Mk. III **is shown** here.

No. 41 Squadron at Northolt was the first to receive Siskin Mk. III aircraft, in May 1924, and the following month No. 111 Squadron was re-equipped at Duxford. These two units alone flew the Mk. III, but in 1927 the much-improved Mk. IIIA made its appearance, and was issued to a total of ten Squadrons. This photograph shows five Siskin Mk. IIIAs with the red bar identification of No. 41 Squadron.

A number of production Siskins were built as dual-control trainers, which was in fact a reversion to the original Mk. II aircraft. All Siskin Squadrons had at least one two-seater for conversion of new pilots, and this variant was also issued to Flying Training Schools. The engine was the standard Jaguar III.

A Siskin Mk. IIIA of No. 43 Squadron. The Mk. IIIA had a re-designed rear fuselage, a reduction of top wing dihedral angle, and was fitted with the supercharged Jaguar IVS engine.

Siskin Mk. IIIA J7176 flying on tropical trials in India, a procedure which was to become standard with new types. In the event, as far as is known, no Siskin units operated at overseas bases during the period of their service. After its return from India, this particular aircraft served at the R.A.F. College, Cranwell.

Siskin IIIA J9895 of No. 43 Squadron taxi-ing out at the Tangmere base. No. 43 were equipped with Siskins from June 1928 and flew in many Hendon Air Displays.

The de Havilland D.H.77 was built to A.M. Specification F.20/27, which called for a new class of "interceptor" fighter, and was powered by the novel 24-cylinder aircooled Napier Rapier engine. The D.H.77 was purchased by the Air Ministry after trials, but not selected for production although it achieved similar performance to the Hawker Hornet (Fury) on 40 per cent less power.

Selected to replace Siskins and Gamecocks, the Bristol Bulldog first entered R.A.F. service in June 1929, when the Mk. II, the production version, was issued to No. 3 Squadron at Upavon. The power unit of all R.A.F. Bulldogs was the Bristol Jupiter VIIF of 490 h.p. No. 3 Squadron marking was a green bar on fuselage and upper wing.

The second unit to re-equip with the Bulldog was No. 17 Squadron in October 1929, again at Upa During the re-equipment period, the Squadron acquired some aircraft from No. 3, hence the mixture of g bar and black zig-zag markings seen in this formation photograph. The first 48 aircraft delivered wer Mk. IIs.

Above and below: Bristol Bulldog Mk. IIAs of No. 17 Squadron. The Mk. IIA (K1603 onwards) featured strengthened structure, increased loaded weight, re-designed oil system, and a wider-track undercarriage with larger tyres. Later changes introduced a modified fin, a tailwheel in place of the skid, and Bendix brakes.

Above: A Bulldog Mk. IIA of No. 23 Squadron. The unit marking of red and blue squares does not show clearly, but the Fighter Squadron eagle motif on the fin carries the Squadron number. Below: A No. 56 Squadron Bulldog Mk. IIA running-up its engine. This Squadron received Bulldogs in October 1932 at North Weald.

Pilots and aircraft of 32 Squadron. These Bulldogs are the later Mk. IIAs, the Squadron having re-equipped in January 1931 at Kenley and moved to Biggin Hill in the following year. During its service, the Bulldog comprised almost three-quarters of the total R.A.F. Fighter strength, the last aircraft being withdrawn in 1937.

Five No. 3 Squadron Bulldogs make an impressive sight as they run in over Hendon for a display, trailing red, white, and blue smoke. These annual displays were a great "showcase" for the R.A.F., and far from being a light-hearted activity, called for a high standard of training and aircraft maintenance. They also enhanced Service recruiting to a considerable degree.

o. 41 Squadron Bulldog testing its air display smoke-generating apparatus, in which micals were injected into the exhaust system to produce smoke trails of varying colour. practice, inspired by the "sky-writing" of the 1920s, continues to the present day, is used to great effect by air display teams such as the "Red Arrows".

Above and below: Bulldogs of No. 19 Squadron flying in formation from Duxford. In both cases the unit is being led by the Officer Commanding, whose machine has the blue and white check markings applied to fin and elevators.

Above and below: Bulldogs
of No. 17 Squadron flying
from Upavon. These two
views are of the same
formation illustrated on
an earlier page, and
some ex-No. 3 Squadron
aircraft are included
in the formation.

Bulldog Mk. IIA aircraft bearing the red and white checks of No. 56 Squadron and fitted with experimental Townend Ring cowlings. This type of cowling was also fitted to the Boulton Paul Overstrand and the Saro London flying-boat. By a coincidence, the nearest aircraft bears the original serial, K2227, as used on the re-built Bulldog which was crashed at Farnborough in 1963.

Bulldog Mk. IIA J9574 of No. 3 Squadron taxi-ing out during the 1930 Hendon Air Display, in which the unit made an impressive and spirited attack on a ground setpiece. The No. 3 aircraft, apart from their highly-polished cowlings, were rendered even more colourful by a green fuselage top decking.

Bulldog Mk. IIA K2210 of No. 19 Squadron comes to grief after a forced landing in a deceptively-smooth field. The aircraft must have been completely inverted at one stage, for the top of the rudder is damaged. The Bulldog was a very strong aircraft, a fact amply demonstrated by pilot survival in the 1963 Farnborough crash of K2227!

In September 1935, No. 3 Squadron took its Bulldogs to the Sudan to be ready for any eventualities following Mussolini's action in Abyssinia. Three of the unit's aircraft are seen here in flight over typical terrain,
from their base at Khartoum, where an open cockpit must have proved a blessing! No. 3 returned to the U.K.
in August 1936.

A good close-up of a Bulldog, probably of No. 41 Squadron. The close proximity of the
general public, and the presence of other aircraft types would seem to indicate that the
occasion was one of the popular Open Days or Empire Air days, when airfields would be
thrown open to visitors and a flying display presented.

64

As with the Grebe and the Siskin, a number of Bulldogs, fifty-eight altogether, were built as two-seat dual-control trainers, the prototype being K2188. The Bulldog Trainers were issued to the Central Flying School, the R.A.F. College at Cranwell, and to various Flying Training Schools, for instruction and conversion.

The prototype Gloster Gauntlet was developed from a long line of fighter biplanes, including the Grebe and Gamecock, and began life as the S.S. 18 (Mercury or Jupiter engine). In 1930, an Armstrong Siddeley Panther engine was fitted, and the aircraft redesignated S.S. 18B. Then, in 1931, reversion was made to the Jupiter engine as the S.S. 19. In 1932, the engine was changed to a Mercury VIS, and with the designation of S.S. 19B this original airframe (J9125) became the true Gauntlet prototype.

The first production Gauntlets were delivered to No. 19 Squadron in May 1935 at Duxford and their wheel fairings were soon removed, due to ingress of mud and grass. The aircraft seen here (K5297) is a Gauntlet II of No. 66 Squadron at Duxford, originally owned by No. 56. The Gauntlet II featured structural modifications.

The prototype Gauntlet in flight, fitted with a 570 h.p. VIS2 engine and improved Townend ring cowling. In this state, J9125 achieved 215 m.p.h. at 16,500 feet.

A Gauntlet II at North Coates, fitted with a three-blade Fairey fixed-pitch propeller which was a feature of many late-production aircraft.

68

A line-up of Gauntlets at North Weald, bearing the red and white checks of No. 56 Squadron, who flew the type from May 1936 to July 1937, when they re-equipped with the Gladiator. The Gauntlet was extremely popular with all Squadron pilots, for it was a fine aerobatic aircraft with a performance to match.

An unusual view of a Gauntlet looping, with the sun catching its under-surfaces. The Gauntlet had a claim to fame, stemming from the fact that aircraft of No. 32 Squadron were the first R.A.F. fighters to make a radar-directed interception—on an unsuspecting airliner over the Thames in 1937.

Gauntlet K7843 displays the red arrowhead marking of No. 46 Squadron, a device derived from the Squadron badge. No. 46 was formed from "B" Flight of No. 17 Squadron at Kenley on 3 September 1936, moving its Gauntlets to Digby in the following year, where it finally re-equipped with Hurricanes in March 1939.

The last of the R.A.F. biplane fighters, the Gloster Gladiator was developed from the Gauntlet, and the prototype, seen here, made its first flight in September 1934 as the Gloster S.S.37, powered by a Bristol Mercury engine. The original open cockpit may be noted. Early production aircraft were fitted with a two-bladed propeller.

The Gladiator prototype, K5200, seen in flight. At this time, the underwing guns were of the Vickers K type; in production the Gladiator was armed with four .303-inch Brownings, two in the fuselage and two in the wings. The undercarriage was fitted with Dowty streamlined and internally-sprung wheels.

The first unit to receive the Gladiator was No. 72 Squadron, which was reformed at Tangmere on 22 March 1937 from a flight of No. 1 Squadron. No. 72's marking was a blue band, edged at top and bottom by red. Gladiator I K6143 of this unit is shown here at Farnborough during the 1937 Air Exercises, with Squadron markings deleted.

A total of thirty-one R.A.F. Squadrons were equipped with the Gladiator, and many saw service at the beginning of World War II. No. 247 Squadron was operational in the Battle of Britain, and others served in Norway, France, Malta, Aden, and the Western Desert, also in Greece, with considerable success against more modern enemy machines.

Above: A flight of three Gladiators, probably belonging to No. 56 Squadron, as the lead aircraft, K8000, is listed as serving with that unit. Below: K7985 of No. 73 Squadron displays the unit marking of a blue diamond with yellow centre stripe. No. 73 was based at Debden and Digby in 1937 and 1938 with Gladiators.

Together with many other historic aircraft, several examples of the Gladiator are still in existence. K8032 is shown here flying at an air display in recent times, having been rebuilt from the components of several surviving airframes and engines to a flying state. It carries the green marking of No. 3 Squadron.

Gladiator K6145, an early production aircraft of No. 3 Squadron. Note that the green unit marking, originally a band, has now become stylised. No. 3 Squadron was the second unit to receive these aircraft, in March 1937.

The unnamed Hawker F.20/27, with a Mercury engine, was built as a private venture, using its title Specification (for an interceptor fighter) as a guide. Its design, however, incorporated the ability to fit the new Rolls-Royce F.XI in-line engine. This aircraft, J9123, is seen above. Below is the second prototype, J9682, with the Rolls-Royce engine. This aircraft, at first known as the Hornet, was re-named as the Hawker Fury I.

During its trials at Martlesham Heath, the Fury made a great impression on all concerned, and the type was chosen as the standard R.A.F. interceptor, 117 being built between 1930 and 1935, powered by what was now the Rolls-Royce Kestrel IIS engine. No. 43 Squadron at Tangmere was the first to receive the Fury. The second production aircraft is shown here.

Above: Fury I of the R.A.F. College, Cranwell, shows off its fine lines in flight. This was the first R.A.F. fighter to exceed 200 m.p.h. in level flight, and probably the ultimate in biplane fighter design. Below: Three Furies display the black band marking of No. 2 Squadron, which equipped with the type in 1932. The last aircraft is the Naval version the Nimrod.

81

Above: Fury I K37?
of No. 5 Flying Trai
School. Only three
Squadrons were
equipped with the
Fury I: Nos 1 and 4
at Tangmere, and
No. 25 at Hawkinge
This was largely d
to previous accept
of the Bulldog, and
thus the Furies
became the spearh
of Britain's air defe
force. Below: An
unusual view of a
Fury, as K5669 has
twin Vickers guns
tested at the butts
R.A.F. Sealand.

ove: A later view of
36 of No. 5 F.T.S.
wn on opposite
e). The aircraft has
n re-painted in
her yellow, from
original silver,
has acquired a
wheel and main-
el brakes. Below:
I K2070 of No. 25
adron. The tail of
62, just visible to
left, bears the 25
adron badge on a
ured tail-fin,
tifying a Flight
mmander's aircraft.

Furies of No. 1
Squadron display an
impeccable line-abrea
formation, and show
off the red bars of
their unit marking.
The Furies of all thre
Squadrons became
star performers at th
annual Hendon show
and No. 1's best-
remembered contribu
tion was the four-
aircraft formation
aerobatic team, unde
the leadership of Flt.
Lt. E. M. Donaldson.
This team also
performed at the Zuri
International Air
Meeting to great effe

In 1934, the R.A.F. Station at Bircham Newton was honoured by a visit from King George V and Queen Mary to view a flying and ground display. In this photograph, the Station Commander, Wg. Cmdr. Raymond Collishaw, is seen on the King's left, while Queen Mary inspects a Fury of No. 1 Squadron. The other aircraft in the line-up are Fairey Gordons, with the nose of an Avro Tutor in the right foreground. The uniforms worn still have R.F.C. influence.

Two Fury II aircraft, believed to be of No. 41 Squadron. This improved variant had a Kestrel VI engine of 640 h.p. in place of the original 525 h.p. unit, and streamlined spats on the wheels. As a result, the all-round performance significantly improved, and the Fury II was ordered into quantity production, entering service with No. 25 Squadron in December 1936. The type also equipped Nos. 41, 43, 73 and 87 Squadrons, Flying Training Schools, and the South African Air Force.

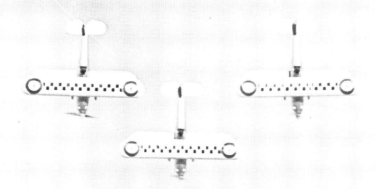

Three Fury I aircraft of No. 43 Squadron diving after looping in formation. This Squadron flew Furies from May 1931 until November 1938, and in the latter part of this period, Fury Is and IIs were in service at the same time.

A Fury II of No. 25 Squadron in the hangar for a rigging check. K7271 was a Flight Commander's aircraft, with the fin painted in the Flight colour and carrying the Squadron badge.

To explore the possibilities of future Fury development, Hawkers built two aircraft as a private venture, the first being civil-registered as G-ABSE and known as the Intermediate Fury. The second prototype is shown here, serialled K3586 as the High Speed Fury. This aircraft first flew on 3 May 1933, and carried out many hours of experimental flying with various Marks of the Kestrel and Goshawk engines.

Built at the Belgian factory of the Fairey company in 1936, the Fairey Feroce was developed from the earlier Fantome fighter and powered by a 925 h.p. Hispano-Suiza engine, the aircraft being armed with four machine-guns. One aircraft was supplied to the Air Ministry as L7045, but no production order transpired.

The High Speed Fury fitted with tapered wings and Vee struts, as opposed to the straight wings seen in the view on the preceding page. The latter configuration was used with the Goshawk engines, in combination with condensers on the leading edges of the upper wing. For most of its life, K3586 had tapered wings.

An impressive view of No. 25 Squadron Fury II aircraft in starboard echelon formation. The leading machine bears the Commanding Officer's pennant just behind the cockpit, and has a coloured fin and tailplane, the usual mark of the C.O.'s personal mount in fighter units.

Two photographs of the High Speed Fury in 1934, registered to Hawkers for experimental flying as the I-PV3. The upper view shows the machine with the Goshawk engine and upper wing leading edge condensers, the wing in th case having sweepback. The lower view is of the aircraft with one of severa marks of Kestrel power un fitted, plus a more normal top wing. Altogether, the High Speed Fury cost £12,000 in manufacture an development, but provided much useful data.

In 1931, the superior performance of the Hawker Hart light bomber influenced the Air Ministry to specify (Spec. 15/30) for a fighter variant, thus reviving the two-seat fighter concept of World War I. The Hart Fighter prototype is shown here, and first production machines were issued to one Flight of No. 23 Squadron in March 1931. In July 1932 the type was re-named as the Demon.

The Hart Fighter, fitted with an experimental windscreen for the pilot and gunner, which was not adopted. The machine was armed with two fixed guns forward and one free gun aft, and the power unit was the Kestrel IIS or Kestrel V (de-rated).

Hawker Demon K3776, listed as being on charge to No. 41 Squadron, which received Demons in July 1934 at Northolt and the following year took them out to Aden. Altogether, 234 Demons were built for the R.A.F. by Hawkers and Boulton Paul at Kingston and Wolverhampton, and the type served with twelve Squadrons of the R.A.F. and Auxiliary Air Force.

From October 1936, all Demons produced by the Boulton Paul factory were fitted with Frazer-Nash hydraulic turrets for the gunner, and thus became the Demon(T), of which K5698 of No. 23 Squadron, shown here, is an example.

Above: In this photograph of No. 23 Squadron Demons, the nearest aircraft to the camera is K5698, illustrated on the preceding page, but it now carries the Squadron marking of red and blue squares. Below: A line-up of new Demon(T) aircraft of No. 23 Squadron, probably photographed in the spring of 1937, when these aircraft arrived.

Above: Demon K2857, an early production aircraft originally issued to No. 23 Squadron, but now relegated to target-towing duties and painted in the garish yellow and black colour scheme authorised for this work. Below: Hastily-applied camouflage, deleted serials, and Squadron code of MS for No. 23 in the Munich Crisis of 1938.

Air combat *circa* 1933. A Demon fighter dives to the attack on a Handley Page Heyford bomber in the Annual Air Exercises of November 1933. These exercises were extremely comprehensive, with a division of Home Squadrons into attackers and defenders, and provided the Air Staff with a good insight of operational efficiency, co-operation, and a general picture of existing United Kingdom air defence.